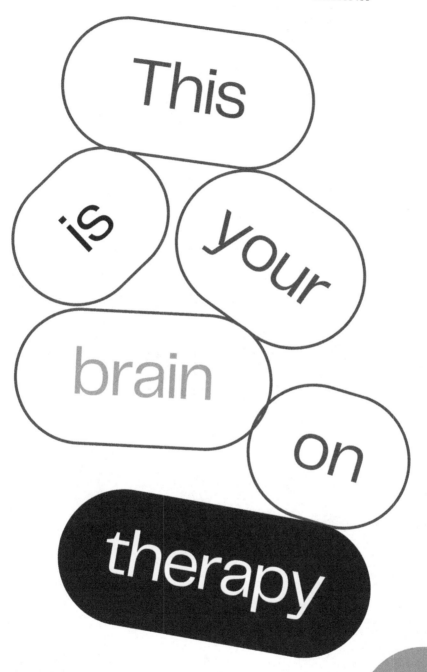

This is your brain on therapy

a record of personal transformation

Grab a pen

You're gonna need it.

Table of Contents

This is your brain on therapy — 5

How this journal works — 6

Questions to ponder — 7

Goals — 11

Session notes — 13

Go deeper — 116

Final Questions — 141

Resources — 145

Who made this journal? — 146

Therapy works when you do

(and you're already on your way).

This is your brain on therapy

Therapy has the power to help change the way you think, feel, live, and love. This promising transformation is not freely given, however. It's earned. The essential ingredients: a belief that change is possible, a commitment to radical honesty with yourself and your trusted guide, and the courage to take action on your insights.

Lasting change requires not only talking about what's bothering you, but *translating* your insights into new ways of thinking and acting, and intentional, mindful practice. To reinforce the work you're doing in therapy, WRITE! Jot down what happens in session, what matters to you, and what you want to work on. Use the blank pages to go deeper. **Tell your truth, read it back, reflect, take action, and repeat.**

Added bonus: according to a recent Harvard Business study, people who write down their goals are 10 times more successful in achieving them.

Human beings have this incredible capacity to become free of unhelpful thoughts, emotions, and beliefs that shape the way we see ourselves and the world. But it's impossible to do this work alone. We need each other, and we need safe spaces to express ourselves as we grow. This journal is a place to document your evolution. Soon, it will be a record of your very own personal transformation. **Let's do this.**

How this journal works

Think of *This is your Brain on Therapy* as your pint-sized therapeutic companion. Grab a pen and get into it before, during, and/or after your sessions. Use it before to get clear on what you want to discuss, and review progress on any goals you've set. Use it during to jot down insights, ideas and anything you want to be sure to remember. And use it afterwards to process, rant, reflect and go deeper. If it's possible, give yourself a 10-minute bumper before and after each therapy session to do this.

IMPORTANT: This is not an English assignment! Give the finger to good form. Write like no one's watching. Write without editing or criticism. Write from heart to hand. Tell the truth and trust yourself.

Use *This is Your Brain on Therapy* to...

- Get focused on why you're in therapy and what you want to change
- Write down important ideas, insights, and mini-goals from each therapy session
- Look deeper and clarify what's underneath your top-of-mind goals
- Track your homework and heartwork from each session
- Journal, rant, reflect, process, doodle, design your future life, etc.
- Review the arc of your progress over weeks and months

Questions to ponder

Consider these questions as you begin using this journal, or anytime you want to reframe your therapy process:

The *Miracle Question*: If you could wake up tomorrow to find your life exactly as you want it, how would it be? What's in the way of this now? What help do you need?

Are you clear about what progress looks and feels like?

Are you ready to be fully seen, beautiful imperfections and all?

Are you aware of your strengths and positive traits, and do you share them in session?

What is your therapist's framework? Does it match what you're trying to achieve?

Have you shared with your therapist what's working (and what's not working) about their approach? **This is super important for you both.**

One more:

How do you want to feel by the end of your journey with this journal?

We've included space for 26 sessions in this book. That's six months of weekly therapy.

"Each of you is perfect the way you are, and you can use a little improvement."

–Shunryu Suzuki

Goals

What specific goals do you want to work on with your therapist? If your therapy isn't goal-oriented, use this page to express why you're using therapy to transform your life, and what you want to explore. You can also use pages in the back of this journal to make your goals more concrete and actionable.

SESSION NOTES

BEFORE

session date

What do you want to focus on during this session?

What do you want to be sure to share?

DURING | AFTER

session date

**What came up during today's session?
What does this mean to you?**

Any homework or heartwork?

What's your biggest takeaway from today?

!

Anything you didn't get to talk about that you want to be sure to bring up next session?

"Nothing ever goes away until it has taught us what we need to know."

-Pema Chodron

BEFORE

session date

What do you want to focus on during this session?

What do you want to be sure to share?

DURING | AFTER

session date

**What came up during today's session?
What does this mean to you?**

Any homework or heartwork?

What's your biggest takeaway from today?

Anything you didn't get to talk about that you want to be sure to bring up next session?

Feelings: real but not always true.

BEFORE

session date

What do you want to focus on during this session?

What do you want to be sure to share?

DURING | AFTER

session date

**What came up during today's session?
What does this mean to you?**

Any homework or heartwork?

What's your biggest takeaway from today?

Anything you didn't get to talk about that you want to be sure to bring up next session?

"We cannot think ourselves into a new way of living – we have to live ourselves into a new way of thinking."

-Claude AnShin Thomas

BEFORE

session date

What do you want to focus on during this session?

What do you want to be sure to share?

DURING | AFTER

session date

**What came up during today's session?
What does this mean to you?**

Any homework or heartwork?

What's your biggest takeaway from today?

Anything you didn't get to talk about that you want to be sure to bring up next session?

"The good life is a process, not a state of being. It is a direction, not a destination."

-Carl Rogers

BEFORE

session date

What do you want to focus on during this session?

What do you want to be sure to share?

DURING | AFTER

session date

**What came up during today's session?
What does this mean to you?**

Any homework or heartwork?

What's your biggest takeaway from today?

Anything you didn't get to talk about that you want to be sure to bring up next session?

"Your vision will become clear only when you look into your heart. Who looks outside, dreams. Who looks inside, awakens."

–Carl Jung

BEFORE

session date

What do you want to focus on during this session?

What do you want to be sure to share?

DURING | AFTER

session date

**What came up during today's session?
What does this mean to you?**

Any homework or heartwork?

What's your biggest takeaway from today?

Anything you didn't get to talk about that you want to be sure to bring up next session?

"When we are no longer able to change a situation—just think of an incurable disease such as inoperable cancer—we are challenged to change ourselves."

–Viktor E. Frankl

session date

What do you want to focus on during this session?

What do you want to be sure to share?

DURING | AFTER

session date

**What came up during today's session?
What does this mean to you?**

Any homework or heartwork?

What's your biggest takeaway from today?

Anything you didn't get to talk about that you want to be sure to bring up next session?

"We learn by practice. Whether it means to learn to dance by practicing dancing or to learn to live by practicing living, the principles are the same. One becomes in some area an athlete of God."

–Martha Graham

BEFORE

session date

What do you want to focus on during this session?

What do you want to be sure to share?

DURING | AFTER

session date

**What came up during today's session?
What does this mean to you?**

Any homework or heartwork?

What's your biggest takeaway from today?

Anything you didn't get to talk about that you want to be sure to bring up next session?

"It is not primarily our physical selves that limit us, but rather our mindset about our physical limits."

–Ellen J. Langer

BEFORE

session date

What do you want to focus on during this session?

What do you want to be sure to share?

DURING | AFTER

session date

**What came up during today's session?
What does this mean to you?**

Any homework or heartwork?

What's your biggest takeaway from today?

!

Anything you didn't get to talk about that you want to be sure to bring up next session?

BEFORE

session date

What do you want to focus on during this session?

What do you want to be sure to share?

DURING | AFTER

session date

**What came up during today's session?
What does this mean to you?**

Any homework or heartwork?

What's your biggest takeaway from today?

Anything you didn't get to talk about that you want to be sure to bring up next session?

"Meanings are not determined by situations, but we determine ourselves by the meanings we give to situations."

-Alfred Adler

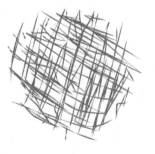

session date

What do you want to focus on during this session?

What do you want to be sure to share?

DURING | AFTER

session date

What came up during today's session? What does this mean to you?

Any homework or heartwork?

What's your biggest takeaway from today?

Anything you didn't get to talk about that you want to be sure to bring up next session?

"What we are doing here is so important, we better not take it too seriously."

−Suzuki Roshi

BEFORE

session date

What do you want to focus on during this session?

What do you want to be sure to share?

DURING | AFTER

session date

What came up during today's session?
What does this mean to you?

Any homework or heartwork?

What's your biggest takeaway from today?

Anything you didn't get to talk about that you want to be sure to bring up next session?

Are your sessions starting to feel the same? What would make them more engaging?

BEFORE

session date

What do you want to focus on during this session?

What do you want to be sure to share?

DURING | AFTER

session date

What came up during today's session? What does this mean to you?

Any homework or heartwork?

What's your biggest takeaway from today?

!

Anything you didn't get to talk about that you want to be sure to bring up next session?

"Challenges are gifts that force us to search for a new center of gravity."

—Oprah Winfrey

BEFORE

session date

What do you want to focus on during this session?

What do you want to be sure to share?

DURING | AFTER

session date

**What came up during today's session?
What does this mean to you?**

Any homework or heartwork?

What's your biggest takeaway from today?

Anything you didn't get to talk about that you want to be sure to bring up next session?

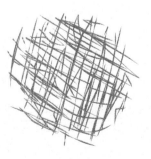

"The wound is the place where the light enters you."

–Rumi

session date

What do you want to focus on during this session?

What do you want to be sure to share?

DURING | AFTER

session date

**What came up during today's session?
What does this mean to you?**

Any homework or heartwork?

What's your biggest takeaway from today?

!

Anything you didn't get to talk about that you want to be sure to bring up next session?

"To have a clear mind but a wild irrepressible heart is one of the keys to human happiness."

–David Whyte

session date

What do you want to focus on during this session?

What do you want to be sure to share?

DURING | AFTER

session date

What came up during today's session?
What does this mean to you?

Any homework or heartwork?

What's your biggest takeaway from today?

Anything you didn't get to talk about that you want to be sure to bring up next session?

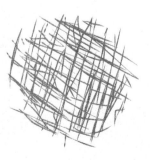

"I am not afraid of storms, for I am learning how to sail my ship."

-Louisa May Alcott

session date

What do you want to focus on during this session?

What do you want to be sure to share?

DURING | AFTER

session date

What came up during today's session? What does this mean to you?

Any homework or heartwork?

What's your biggest takeaway from today?

Anything you didn't get to talk about that you want to be sure to bring up next session?

Trauma is not your fault. Period.

BEFORE

session date

What do you want to focus on during this session?

What do you want to be sure to share?

DURING | AFTER

session date

**What came up during today's session?
What does this mean to you?**

Any homework or heartwork?

What's your biggest takeaway from today?

Anything you didn't get to talk about that you want to be sure to bring up next session?

"If you're always trying to be normal, you will never know how amazing you can be."

-Maya Angelou

BEFORE

session date

What do you want to focus on during this session?

What do you want to be sure to share?

DURING | AFTER

session date

What came up during today's session?
What does this mean to you?

Any homework or heartwork?

What's your biggest takeaway from today?

Anything you didn't get to talk about that you want to be sure to bring up next session?

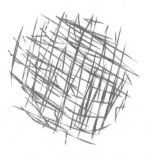

Healing also means taking responsibility for the role you play in your own suffering.

BEFORE

session date

What do you want to focus on during this session?

What do you want to be sure to share?

DURING | AFTER

session date

**What came up during today's session?
What does this mean to you?**

Any homework or heartwork?

What's your biggest takeaway from today?

Anything you didn't get to talk about that you want to be sure to bring up next session?

The best way to find out whether you're on the right path? Stop looking at the path.

-Marcus Buckingham

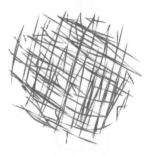

BEFORE

session date

What do you want to focus on during this session?

What do you want to be sure to share?

DURING | AFTER

session date

What came up during today's session? What does this mean to you?

Any homework or heartwork?

What's your biggest takeaway from today?

!

Anything you didn't get to talk about that you want to be sure to bring up next session?

"Almost everything will work again if you unplug it for a few minutes, including you."

–Anne Lamott

BEFORE

session date

What do you want to focus on during this session?

What do you want to be sure to share?

DURING | AFTER

session date

**What came up during today's session?
What does this mean to you?**

Any homework or heartwork?

What's your biggest takeaway from today?

Anything you didn't get to talk about that you want to be sure to bring up next session?

"No amount of anxiety can change the future. No amount of regret can change the past."

— Karen Salmansohn

BEFORE

session date

What do you want to focus on during this session?

What do you want to be sure to share?

DURING | AFTER

session date

**What came up during today's session?
What does this mean to you?**

Any homework or heartwork?

What's your biggest takeaway from today?

Anything you didn't get to talk about that you want to be sure to bring up next session?

"There is something in the human spirit that will survive and prevail, a tiny and brilliant light burning in the heart of mankind that will not go out no matter how dark the world becomes."

–Leo Tolstoy

BEFORE

session date

What do you want to focus on during this session?

What do you want to be sure to share?

DURING | AFTER

session date

What came up during today's session?
What does this mean to you?

Any homework or heartwork?

What's your biggest takeaway from today?

Anything you didn't get to talk about that you want to be sure to bring up next session?

"If you listen to birds, every day will have a song in it."

–Kyo Maclear

BEFORE

session date

What do you want to focus on during this session?

What do you want to be sure to share?

DURING | AFTER

session date

**What came up during today's session?
What does this mean to you?**

Any homework or heartwork?

What's your biggest takeaway from today?

Anything you didn't get to talk about that you want to be sure to bring up next session?

"I will tell you a secret, what is really important: True love is really the same as conscious awareness. They are identical."

—Jack Kornfield

session date

What do you want to focus on during this session?

What do you want to be sure to share?

DURING | AFTER

session date

**What came up during today's session?
What does this mean to you?**

Any homework or heartwork?

What's your biggest takeaway from today?

Anything you didn't get to talk about that you want to be sure to bring up next session?

Go deeper

Use the following pages to expand on your discoveries, reflections, and important takeaways.

Final Questions

How do you feel now that you've completed this journal?

What have you learned? What have you unlearned?

What are you taking with you from this journey?

What do you want to be sure to remember?

What can you share with others that would be of benefit?

Feel free to use the next pages to jot down your answers.

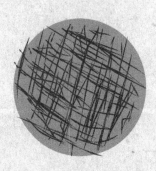

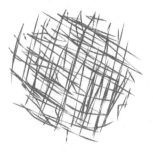

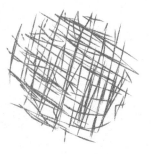

Resources

In a Crisis:

Crisis services provide immediate emotional support and resources to people in distress and their worried family and friends.

National Suicide Prevention and Crisis Hotline: call or text 988

Emergency: 911

National Alliance on Mental Illness 800.540.6264 | Nami.org

Free Guided Meditations:

insighttimer.com

Personal Names and Numbers:

Therapist:

Family members:

Close trusted friends:

Pleased to meet you

Brian Shiers, LMFT

Brian Shiers is a Certified Mindfulness Facilitator, holds a Masters Degree in psychology with a concentration in Interpersonal Neurobiology, and is a Licensed Marriage and Family Therapist. Brian uses mindfulness to create a safe holding environment for treating anxiety disorders, healing attachment wounds, and teaching DBT skills. He is a senior teacher for UCLA's Mindful Awareness Research Center and provides mindfulness programs for clients such as the FBI, Disney Animation Studios, and the UCLA David Geffen School of Medicine.

Learn more at AlignedMindTherapy.com

Laurie Shiers, CPCC

Laurie Shiers is a Certified Professional Co-Active Coach who helps people break through creative and emotional blocks to access the freedom, focus, and courage it takes to finally put themselves—and their ideas--first. She is creator of Creative Block, a tool that artists and entrepreneurs use to get out their own way, and the co-author of the bestselling book, *Mindset Mondays with DTK*. Laurie credits her strong journaling practice and her many productive years in therapy for helping to shape her into the mostly high-functioning person she is today.

Visit Laurie at laurieshiers.com

In case you were wondering, yes, we are married. :)

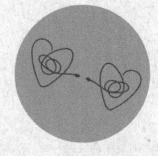

Made in the USA
Las Vegas, NV
23 October 2023

79598905R00083